Pr

PROPHETIC PRAYERS AND INSIGHTS MANUAL

30 Days to a Stronger, More Effective Prayer Life

Thank God for prophets like Laticia Simpson, who will raise up a standard against the works of darkness. I have known Prophet Laticia Simpson for over fifteen years, and her message has always been the same...to raise up a standard against the works of darkness and bring a new sound to the Body of Christ. Prophet Simpson has been given an international assignment to expose the works of the enemy and bring deliverance back to the church. Her experience in contending with spiritual warfare is in high demand all over the world and has made her a treasured jewel in the body of Christ. She will always be a special friend to my family and my churches.

Chaplain (MAJ) Javon Seaborn US ARMY Ret.
Canon Javon Seaborn
Canon for Military Affairs and Chaplaincy
Boga Diocese (Providence of Congo Anglican Communion)

Where do we begin concerning this mighty woman of God? We met her in late 2009 through our military service at Ft. Leavenworth, KS while in ministry together at Faith Christian Center International. One of the first things you must know about our sister is that she is a true prayer warrior!

As a prophet she is keen and is able to be trusted with the secrets of God and others. We have witnessed firsthand God's pleasure to skillfully and masterfully operate through this vessel to call **out**... call **forth**...speak **over**...speak **into**...**fore**tell...and **forth**tell as He desires. She will only speak what the Lord says and she desires to stay in God's presence, and to always know what's on His heart. Anyone who has this vessel in their life is blessed beyond measure.

Preston Gamble, SSG, USA (Retired).
Pastor—Kingdom Life Seekers
Tallahassee, FL
Zipporah Gamble, RN, BSN
Co-Pastor—Kingdom Life Seekers
Tallahassee, FL

The Prophetic Prayers and Insights Manual is one woman's story of victory over a tragic event. Prayer is what kept her during one of the loneliest times of her life. Laticia Simpson is a woman of prayer and it is her strong foundation in prayer that has caused her to experience endless victories. I strongly endorse this book and suggest that you participate in each day's requirement in order to experience victorious living.

Tokoni Cheryle Bush
Pray Woman Pray, Inc., Visionary
Augusta, GA

Laticia Washington has blessed the body of Christ with her knowledge and understanding of the prophetic, and her fresh fire and powerful anointing. Her presence shifts, stimulates and provokes the people of God to an unquenchable hunger and thirst. She is a blessing to all those who are graced with her gifts. Laticia has a fire that burns inside of her and that fire reaches souls all over the world. Her in-depth knowledge of the prophetic brings enlightenment to the body of Christ, and new waves of glory are released wherever she opens her mouth and speaks divine, God-breathed words. This book will help clarify your understanding of the prophetic gift and its ability to increase the faith of all those who are blessed by its' demonstration.

Dr. Michelle Gordon
Restoration Deliverance Ministries, Inc.
Jesup, GA

It is with great excitement and honor that we see the unfolding of a much-needed Kingdom work authored by the spirit of God and produced by Prophetess Laticia Simpson. I have had the pleasure of walking alongside this pioneer in ministry through the avenue of Reveal Kingdom Network, Lions Roar Prophetic Academy, and many other Kingdom advances. The strategy that her life exemplifies is poured out in her intercession. She is a vessel of honor and integrity that models what she professes. Just as she is a living epistle read of men, she transcribes that which God has caused her spirit to conceive to the hearts and minds of His people. Her scribal work is designed to propel the life of the prayerless and the gap filler. A work of deliverance and breakthrough to be noted in the earth. This written work poured out from the heavens will surely leave no stone unturned. Lives are guaranteed to be forever changed.

Apostle Janice Watts
Watts Ministries
Killen, Texas

Prophetess Laticia Simpson and I were stationed in the same unit at Fort Stewart, Georgia and I knew when I met her that we would be friends. Her spirit and personality drew me in as it did with everyone…she is one who never meets a stranger. We quickly got to know one another by sharing our personal stories. We found that we had a considerable amount in common even though we came from different backgrounds. We were both saved yet living a secular lifestyle. We drew closer in friendship throughout the years as deployments and missions continued to make their rounds. Things shifted spiritually in both of our lives when we went on our second deployment to Iraq and became battle buddies. A battle buddy is someone who is paired you with during training and deployments—much like an accountability partner. During these deployments and missions, we saw good days and bad days. Amid them all, the bond we shared kept our spirits high. She always knew how to keep me laughing. I can say without hesitation that she has always recognized God as her Lord and Savior and I believe that is what kept her going. Although we rode the see-saw of fully committing to God, on these deployments we encountered tremendous spiritual growth and eventually rededicated our lives to God.

When Laticia made the decision to fully commit to God on our second deployment, she became a roaring fire for Him. We went from partying to worshipping and praying together. Prayer has always been a part of who she is and she prays for anyone who comes across her path. On one occasion, she began to pray for a gentleman who towered over her. She proceeded to lay hands on the man so hard his knees buckled. It has been an honor to see her spiritually grow in God. She remains consistent and steadfast in her walk with Christ. If you want to know how to effectively pray, she is the person to equip you. She is committed to serving the people of God and committed to the work of the Kingdom. Prophetess Laticia Simpson is a prayer warrior.

Pastor Krishni Ryland
Speak Life Outreach Ministries
Douglasville, GA

This book is a must purchase. Whether you are young in your Christian walk and want to know and learn the voice of God and or are already a prayer warrior or intercessor, you need this book. God has used this woman of God to release the keys to the prophetic realm through this book. This book will raise your prayer life to another level.

Apostle Gossypia Makinwa- Shinault
Preparing the Way For The Lord Ministries INC and
Journey Outreach Ministries INC
Glennville, GA

PROPHETIC PRAYERS
AND
INSIGHTS MANUAL

30 Days to a Stronger, More Effective Prayer Life

Laticia Simpson

Prophetic Prayers and Insights Manual: 30 Days to a Stronger, More Effective Prayer Life
by Laticia Simpson

Cover design, editing, book layout, and publishing services by KishKnows Inc. Richton Park, Illinois, 708-252-DOIT admin@kishknows.com, www.kishknows.com

ISBN - 978-0-578-77664-4
LCCN - 2020921241

Some Scripture references may be paraphrased versions or illustrative references of the author. Unless otherwise specified, all other references are from **King James Version of the Bible**.

Scriptures marked **NIV** are taken from **THE HOLY BIBLE, NEW INTERNATIONAL VERSION®, (NIV)®** Copyright© 1973, 1978, 1984, 2011 by Biblica, Inc.® Used by permission. All rights reserved worldwide.

Scriptures marked **ESV** are taken from **The Holy Bible, English Standard Version (ESV)**, adapted from the Revised Standard Version of the Bible, copyright Division of Christian Education of the National Council of the Churches of Christ in the U.S.A. All rights reserved.

Table of Contents

Dedication

"Pray without ceasing"
1 Thessalonians 5:17

This book is dedicated to YOU. My prayer is that you will become brave and confident, strengthening your prayer life and seeing the answers to your prayers manifest before your eyes.

I wanted to write this prayer manual because prayer is the key to having an open dialogue with the Father, constant communication in the spirit realm, and revelation. It is the key that unlocks doors. I want to encourage you to never leave this number one principle out of your life. Without prayer, how can you have a relationship with God? In order to have a relationship with anyone, you must *communicate*. This manual is to help you give God His Word back, and believe in what you release to Him that it should happen. It's like being reminded of something you have said—it holds you accountable. The Lord is accountable, and His Word cannot return unto Him void. This manual is to train, equip, and encourage you to pray with power, and believe in the One who answers your prayers.

I also hope that after reading these powerful but simple strategies, your prayer life will be stronger than it was before. I pray that you will be bold and confident in your faith, so that what you speak shall come to pass without doubting.

Be Blessed!

Acknowledgments

I want to first and foremost thank God, without whom I would not be here.

Thank you to…

- **My family**, for believing in the God in me.
- **My husband**, who pushes me beyond my boundaries and is my biggest champion.
- **My children**, who encourage me daily to be a better version of myself.
- **My friends**, who remind me that I have purpose, and that there are people waiting on what I must deliver.

These are the people behind why this prayer manual had to be written, and why my words must be unique and from the heart.

Thank you.

The Foundation

Day One

"Her children arise and call her blessed..."
Proverbs 31:28a (NIV)

My story...
Prayer was always a part of my mother's life. I remember as a child, hearing my mother in her bathroom praying and crying. Her bathroom was huge—you could lay down on the floor and stretch out while you talked to the Lord. I didn't understand why...but I knew she was talking to God. I used to think that she was crazy...and then I started seeing the things that she was praying about getting better.

A mother's privilege...
Since the beginning of time, mothers have been on their knees in prayer. We pray for safety. For the resources to care for our children. For Him to bring back the wayward ones. Our finances, our relationships, our jobs, our families...we pray in the car. In the kitchen, as we rock our babies, and even in the bathroom, where we can stretch out and talk to the Lord. No matter where we are, we can be assured that He is listening...and that things are going to get better.

Think about it...
Where is your favorite place to pray? What is it about this place that you like? Describe it here in a sentence or two.

_____

_____

_____

_____

_____

_____

_____

_____

Day Two

"For where two or three are gathered in my name, there am I among them."
Matthew 18:20 (NIV)

My story...

I was brought up in a little Baptist church with about twenty-five members. We would go and read a few Scriptures, and sing a few hymns. The preacher would give a short sermon that sometimes we understood and sometimes we didn't, and then we would go home...and that was church.

It's the size of the prayers, not the size of the church...

God isn't looking for the biggest church. He isn't judging our prayers by how many people are praying with us. He's looking at the heart. Whether your church has twenty-five members or 25,000...or it's just you, flat out in your bathroom, crying out to the Lord, know this: *He hears you.* The noise of the world cannot drown you out. And He comes running when you call.

Think about it...

Did you attend church as a child? What was it like? How does it compare to the church that you attend now? Take some time to write out your thoughts here.

_____

_____

_____

_____

_____

_____

_____

_____

_____

Day Three

*"When you lie down, you will not be afraid;
when you lie down, your sleep will be sweet."*
Proverbs 3:24

My story...

As a little girl, my bedtime prayers were way beyond *"Now I lay me down to sleep."* I prayed for the birds, the cats, and the dogs. Everyone in my family. I told Him about my day at school...who was mean to me and who I wanted Him to "get" for me. Sometimes, I would fall asleep...and when I woke up, I would pick up right where I had left off!

Rest in His arms...

Have you ever fallen asleep while you were praying? I am the first to raise my hand! Were you embarrassed? Think about it this way: *There is no safer place to be than in the arms of your heavenly Father.* You can trust Him to hold your prayers for you while you sleep...and to remember right where you were when you drifted off. Rest easy tonight. He's got you.

Think about it...

When was the last time you fell asleep while you were talking to the Lord? How did you feel when you woke up? Write your thoughts here.

_____

_____

_____

_____

_____

_____

_____

_____

_____

Day Four

"How long, Lord? Will you forget me forever?
How long will you hide your face from me?"
Psalm 13:1 (NIV)

My story...

Have you ever fussed at God? I have done so plenty of times when I felt mistreated or abused. As I got older, I realized that when I thought my mother was angry, she was actually just having a conversation with the Lord. And what sounded like "fussing" was her way of crying out to Him, asking Him to answer her when she called.

It's okay to fuss!

The Lord can handle our emotions: our joy, our elation, our sadness, our anger...and our fussing! Our heavenly Father listens to us. He hears us. And while the answers may not be what we are looking for at the time, we can rest in the knowledge that He knows what is best for us and will bring it about in His time.

Think about it...

Have you ever fussed at the Lord? What were you fussing about? Recall the situation and jot down some thoughts here.

_____

_____

_____

_____

_____

_____

_____

_____

_____

_____

Day Five

"So then neither the one who plants nor the one who waters is anything, but God who causes the growth."
1 Corinthians 3:7 (NIV)

My story...
Did you know that by growing up in an environment of prayer, you could have a seed of prayer planted within you? And even if you grew up in a toxic environment, that doesn't mean that you don't have the seed of prayer...it may just need to be watered.

The prayers of the faithful...
There is a quote that says, *"Your grandmother's prayers are still protecting you."* (Lalah Delia) Growing up under the cover of prayer—even if we didn't know it—can have a profound effect on our life. It is comforting to know that the Lord is watching over us before we ever come to know Him!

Think about it...
Was there someone who prayed for you when you were growing up? Write them a letter, and tell them how much their prayers mean to you as an adult.

_____
_____
_____
_____
_____
_____
_____
_____
_____
_____
_____

Day Six

"...for thereby some have entertained angels unawares."
Hebrews 13:2b (KJV)

My story...

Maybe you are familiar with the Bible verse about entertaining angels. As I got older, I realized that it is possible to entertain both angels of light *and* angels of darkness. I began to pay close attention to what was happening and spent more time talking to the Lord about it.

Cultivating a heart of hospitality...

No one is able to meet all of their needs alone. We need each other. As Christians, it is important that we nurture and care for one another. This does not mean that we let anyone who knocks at our door enter in though. The Scriptures tell us to be *"wise as serpents and innocent as doves." (Matthew 10:16 KJV)* We must learn to discern who is safe for us and who is not.

Think about it...

Were there people in your circle growing up that you knew were safe? What made them so? List some of their traits here.

_____
_____
_____
_____
_____
_____
_____
_____
_____
_____
_____
_____

Day Seven

My story...

When I was eleven years old, I was violated by someone that I thought I could trust...someone that I thought loved me. I remember crying, asking why it happened to me and wondering who I could tell about it. I had to realize it was all in the Master's plan. Knowing this made it clear that my pain was for a purpose, understanding that it was a different story than the one I wanted...and that was okay.

When life goes sideways...

Things don't always turn out like we want them to. As we get older, it is easier for us to understand that but as children, it can be really difficult to comprehend why things happen the way they do...and why some things can't be fixed. It is important for our children to know that they can come to us with their problems...no matter what.

Think about it...

Have you ever been in a situation where something happened and you felt like you couldn't tell anyone? Take some time to remember how that felt.

_____

_____

_____

_____

_____

_____

_____

_____

Day Eight

"But I say unto you, love your enemies, bless them that curse you, do good to them that hate you, and pray for them which despitefully use you, and persecute you."
Matthew 5:44 (KJV)

My story...
After the abuse, I felt rejected—like no one loved me. Being hurt and rejected by someone that I trusted and loved was very frightening. I felt alone, like I was targeted for whatever bad things would come along after that. I didn't understand that I still have to love those that hurt me...even though it was not easy.

Forgiveness is a choice...
It is easier to say, *"I forgive you"* than it is to forget what happened. But I would challenge you to try and forget the pain. Let the act of forgiveness erase the hurt, pain, disappointment, and fear, so that you may truly move past it and into a brighter future. Be patient with others, because not everyone walks the same road.

Think about it...
Have you ever experienced rejection through physical or emotional abuse from someone that you thought loved you?
Take some time to journal your thoughts or memories here.

_____

_____

_____

_____

_____

_____

_____

_____

Day Nine

"For the battle is not yours, but God's"
2 Chronicles 20:15b (NIV)

My story...

The abuse started innocently enough, as these things do. I would kiss him goodbye on the lips—then it escalated. If I needed something, he would try to make me kiss him or touch me inappropriately before he would give it to me. I started avoiding him and going without things because I was frightened and never knew what to expect.

In the eye of the storm...

Sometimes, when we find ourselves in an overwhelming situation, the only thing we know to do is to avoid it. This isn't always the wrong response...but it cannot be the solution. Eventually, we have to face it. Sometimes, it looks like saying something else...and sometimes, it looks like confronting it head-on. What we need to remember is the battle belongs to the Lord.

Think about it...

Are you avoiding someone or something right now? How can you confront the situation and move past it? Write down your thoughts here.

_____
_____
_____
_____
_____
_____
_____
_____
_____

Day Ten

"And this is the confidence that we have in him, that if we ask any-
thing according to his will, he heareth us."
1 John 5:14-15 (KJV)

My story...
In our home, we didn't talk about things that happened
with *anyone*—no matter how bad it was. Since I did not feel
like I could talk to anyone about what was happening, I started
talking to Jesus. I heard my mother saying things like, *"Jesus, if*
you don't do it," "Jesus, I can't make it without you," "Jesus, I need
money to pay this bill," "Jesus, keep my child safe," "Jesus, I feel like I
can't get ahead," and *"Help me!"* and I started talking to Him like
I heard her doing.

Teach me, and I remember...
Children learn about the world from their parents. They see
what we do and hear what we say, and their earliest form of
expression is rooted in our actions and words. If they grow up
watching and hearing us pray, they will learn to talk to the Lord
just like they talk to their parents. And that is a priceless gift.

Think about it...
What is the very first prayer you remember praying as a child?
Write the words down here...and go back to being a child at the
feet of Jesus for just a moment.

_____

_____

_____

_____

_____

_____

_____

Day Eleven

"Cast all your anxiety on him because he cares for you."
1 Peter 5:7 (NIV)

My story...

Finally, the day came when I knew I had to tell someone. I called my mother and asked her to come home immediately, because someone had hurt me. My abuser told me that she would not believe me...but I knew in my heart that she would. Imagine the pain when she questioned my story.

The pain of betrayal...

There is perhaps no pain so great as the pain that comes when we are betrayed by someone we love...especially if that person is our parent. We must cling to the hope that we have in Jesus... and remember that while our earthly parents may fail us, our heavenly Father will *always* be there, no matter what.

Think about it...

Do you have a story that you are still struggling to tell because you don't think anyone will believe you? Write it here. If you are comfortable sharing it with someone then do so...if not, then keep it between you and Jesus. He will hold it close for you...and He will *never* betray you.

_____
_____
_____
_____
_____
_____
_____
_____
_____
_____

Day Twelve

"When I am afraid, I put my trust in you."
Psalm 56:3 (NIV)

My story...
Being told that I could not talk about it only reinforced my feelings of rejection and shame. What happened in our house stayed in our house, and I knew that there would be consequences if I spoke about it outside of our family.

Secrets...
Some secrets are good...a Christmas present, an engagement ring...these are the secrets that we keep because we want to surprise someone. Sometimes, secrets can be harmful though. And things that are kept in the dark have a way of taking on a life of their own. But we must remember that there are no secrets from God...He knows everything about us.

Think about it...
Have you ever been asked to keep a secret that made you uncomfortable? Talk about how it made you feel to be the secret keeper. Did you eventually have to talk to someone? What happened when you did?

_____

_____

_____

_____

_____

_____

_____

_____

_____

_____

Day Thirteen

"And you will know the truth, and the truth will set you free."
John 8:32 (NIV)

My story...

My mother went to some family members for advice, not knowing that they had experienced the same thing as a child growing up. The blame was placed on me, saying that some girls are "fast," implying that I had done something to invite the abuse.

Denial is an empty vessel...

Many women who have experienced abuse either block it out or deny that it happened...but denying the truth never helps you heal. You must admit that it happened in order to deal with it. *"Silence is a lie that screams at the light."* (Shannon L. Adler) If we are to find healing, we must first find our voice.

Think about it...

What would it look like for you to "break your silence." Is there someone that you want to talk to, to clear the air over things that have happened in the past? Journal your thoughts here and *find your voice.*

_____
_____
_____
_____
_____
_____
_____
_____
_____
_____
_____

Day Fourteen

"Get rid of all bitterness, rage and anger, brawling and slander, along with every form of malice. Be kind and compassionate to one another, forgiving each other, just as in Christ God forgave you."
Ephesians 4:31-32 (NIV)

My story...

I learned later in life, when I began to process what had happened, that "taking it to the grave" was not going to allow me to heal. The abuse never leaves, but acknowledging what happened and learning to forgive was the key to my healing.

Forgiveness is a choice...

Forgiving someone for the pain that they have caused us is a choice—but it is not always an easy choice. Corrie ten Boom said, after nearly dying in a Nazi concentration camp, *"Forgiveness is an act of the will, and the will can function regardless of the temperature of the heart."* Sometimes, we have to make the hard choice to forgive, even when our heart is still wounded. Jesus forgave us as He hung on the cross...how can we do any less?

Think about it...

Is there someone that you need to forgive? Not the little forgiveness like "She forgot my birthday." The *big* forgiveness; the one that has kept your heart cold and angry. Write them a letter, and *Let. It. Go.*

_____

_____

_____

_____

_____

_____

_____

_____

Day Fifteen

"In my distress I called upon the LORD, and cried unto my God: he heard my voice out of his temple, and my cry came before him, even into his ears."
Psalm 186:6 (NIV)

My story...
All I knew was that I wanted the pain to end. The disappointment...the hurt...the thoughts of harming myself...the feeling of being unloved...I wanted it to end.

When you get to the end of your rope...
We've all seen the meme that says, "When you get to the end of your rope, tie a knot and hold on." Some days, that's easier said than done. One of the simplest and most powerful prayers that we can pray is *"Lord, HELP."* He knows where we are. He's right there, waiting to catch us when we fall.

Think about it...
Have you ever been at the point in your life where you just couldn't take it anymore? What brought you there...and what (or who) brought you out? Take some time to reflect.

_____
_____
_____
_____
_____
_____
_____
_____
_____
_____
_____
_____

Day Sixteen

"As for you, see that what you have heard from the beginning remains in you. If it does, you also will remain in the Son and in the Father."
1 John 2:24 (NIV)

My story...

Even though I had not accepted the Lord yet, I knew deep down that I could talk to Him, and He would listen. My mother's example through the years that I was growing up taught me that I could cry out to Jesus, and He would answer me.

Just as I am...

Have you ever talked to someone about going to church and they responded with some variation of *"I want to, but I need to get my life together first."* Our world has taught us that we should not approach the Father until we are "worthy." But He is waiting right there for us, even before we know Him, to take us in just as we are. There isn't some magic formula to talking to Jesus...just pretend He's sitting right next to you, and tell Him all about it.

Think about it...

Has anything ever held you back from talking to the Lord? What was it? Have you overcome it, or is it still a struggle?

_____
_____
_____
_____
_____
_____
_____
_____
_____
_____

Day Seventeen

"The son said to him, 'Father, I have sinned against heaven and against you. I am no longer worthy to be called your son.'"
Luke 15:21 (NIV)

My story...

I had reached a place where I didn't know anything else to do but pray. I had sought out unhealthy relationships with men, trying to fill a void in my life. My party lifestyle had left me broken and empty, and I know now that God had allowed me to be in those situations so that I, like the Prodigal Son, would come to the end of myself and run to Him. And that is what I did.

Shiny objects...

The things of this world are so...shiny. They draw us in, enticing us with their pleasures and promises...only to leave us broken and empty. God can remove those shiny objects from our vision—but He is waiting for us to realize that we need His help. They will *never* satisfy...He will *forever* satisfy. All we have to do is ask.

Think about it...

Are there "shiny objects" in your life that need to be removed? Have you asked the Lord for help? Take some time to do so now.

_____
_____
_____
_____
_____
_____
_____
_____
_____

Day Eighteen

"Knowing their thoughts, Jesus said, 'Why do you entertain evil thoughts in your hearts?'"
Matthew 9:4 (NIV)

My story...

I was haunted by my secret until I was twenty-five. Part of me would say that I was fine...but my heart knew the truth. I would tell myself that I had forgiven my abuser, but the thought of them made me angry all over again. My life up to that point had been a roller coaster...and I knew that I could not go on that way. I had reached the end of my ability to "handle it."

I'm fine...really...

When someone asks us how we are doing, our automatic response is, "I'm fine." Even when we are the *furthest thing* from being fine. We might be able to fool our friends—but God isn't buying it. He knows that we're not *fine.* And He knows how to make it right...but we have to admit it first. Go ahead. He'll wait.

Think about it...

Is there an area of your life right now that is not "fine?" Reflect on your situation, and ask the Lord to intervene right now. He's listening!

_____
_____
_____
_____
_____
_____
_____
_____

Day Nineteen

"Jesus turned and saw her. 'Take heart, daughter,' he said, 'your faith has healed you.'"
Matthew 9:22 (NIV)

My story...

One night, I attended a church service where the pastor talked about people who were carrying pain and bitterness from being abused, molested, and violated. I felt as though he was speaking right to me. I was sure that he knew exactly what had happened in my life. He said that it was time to give it to God, and let Him heal it...and that is what I did.

Ordinary people, extraordinary message...

God can use the most ordinary people to bring us the most extraordinary message. When He wants to get our attention, He knows just how to do it...and if we aren't listening, He'll talk louder. We cannot outrun God, no matter how hard we try.

Think about it...

Have you ever been in a church service where you felt like the pastor was speaking directly to you, as if you were the only person in the room? What was he telling you?

_____
_____
_____
_____
_____
_____
_____
_____
_____
_____
_____

Day Twenty

"See, I am doing a new thing!
Now it springs up; do you not perceive it?"
Isaiah 43:19a (NIV)

My story...

The pastor said, *"If you are ready to let it go, step into the aisle,"* and I did. The next thing I remember, I was being picked up off of the floor; and even though I didn't remember what had happened, I knew that something had changed. I felt different.

On the floor...

Sometimes, the Lord speaks to us in a "still, small, voice." And sometimes, He needs to speak a little louder to make sure we're listening. Our God is a patient God...but He will take us to the floor...*literally*...if that's what it takes to get our attention.

Think about it...

Have you ever had an encounter with the Lord that literally left you "on the floor?" Where were you, and what was the out-come? Reflect on the details here.

_____

_____

_____

_____

_____

_____

_____

_____

_____

_____

_____

_____

Day Twenty-one

"In peace I will lie down and sleep,
for you alone, Lord,
make me dwell in safety."
Psalm 4:8 (NIV)

My story...
I went home that night...and for the first time in years, I slept like a baby. No nightmares. No fear. I didn't cry myself to sleep as I had done for endless nights before that. I didn't know what had happened...but I knew that *something* had happened...and that things were going to be different. A spark of hope was ignited in my soul that night.

Sweet dreams...
If you've ever had trouble sleeping, then you know how frustrating and frightening it can be. Sleep is supposed to renew our minds and our bodies; and when our fears creep in and hijack our sleep, that doesn't happen. Releasing the fear that keeps our sleep restless and angry can also free our souls and allows us to find hope, perhaps for the first time.

Think about it...
Have you ever had trouble sleeping? What was causing it? And how did you (can you) release it?

_____
_____
_____
_____
_____
_____
_____
_____
_____

Day Twenty-two

"One plants, one waters, and GOD gives the increase."
1 Corinthians 3:7 (NIV)

My story...
Something changed in me that night. I had taken the first step toward healing. I knew that my mother's example of prayer when I was growing up and my own childish prayers had led me to the feet of the Lord.

Think about it...
It is time for you to come to the feet of the Lord. Write a prayer to Him here. Only you know what is on your heart, and this is just between you and your heavenly Father.

_____

_____

_____

_____

_____

_____

_____

_____

_____

_____

_____

_____

_____

_____

_____

_____

_____

_____

_____

The Importance of Prayer

Day Twenty-three

"Let us then with confidence draw near to the throne of grace, that we may receive mercy and find grace to help in time of need."
Hebrews 4:16 (ESV)

Why is prayer important?

Prayer reveals your heart…and the heart of God concerning you. You may be thinking that you do not know how to pray. Sometimes, we can make prayer too deep…and while it is not always deep, it *is* intimacy. Prayer causes a release *in* your life and *for* your life.

Think about it…

Did you grow up with prayer in your home? Were you taught to pray, or did you learn by watching and listening? How has your childhood experience with prayer (or the lack of it) affected your ability to talk to the Lord today?

_____

_____

_____

_____

_____

_____

_____

_____

_____

_____

_____

_____

_____

_____

_____

Day Twenty-four

"And it came to pass, that, as he was praying in a certain place, when he ceased, one of his disciples said unto him, 'Lord, teach us to pray, as John also taught his disciples.' And he said unto them, 'When ye pray, say, "Our Father which art in heaven, Hallowed be thy name. Thy kingdom come. Thy will be done, as in heaven, so in earth. Give us day by day our daily bread. And forgive us our sins; for we also forgive everyone one that is indebted to us. And lead us not into temptation; but deliver us from evil."'
Luke 11:1-4 (NIV)

Think about it...
The Lord's Prayer is as familiar as our own name to most of us. Are there other prayers that you grew up with that bring you comfort? The "Now I Lay Me Down to Sleep" prayer? Or perhaps, your family had their own special prayer for bedtime or for saying grace at dinner. Write the words down here, and revisit your childhood.

_____

_____

_____

_____

_____

_____

_____

_____

_____

_____

_____

_____

_____

_____

_____

_____

Day Twenty-five

"This is the confidence we have in approaching God: that if we ask anything according to his will, he hears us."
1 John 5:14 (NIV)

How do I know God hears me?
You must...

- *Believe He **exists**.*

- *Believe He **answers**.*

- *Have **faith**.*

- *Have **confidence** that what you ask shall be given.*

Think about it...
Take the four points above, and find a Scripture verse that affirms each one.

_____

_____

_____

_____

_____

_____

_____

_____

_____

_____

_____

_____

_____

_____

_____

_____

Day Twenty-six

*"But without faith it is impossible to please him: for he that cometh
to God must believe that he is, and that he is a rewarder of them that
diligently seek him."*
Hebrews 11:6 (NIV)

What if I don't understand the Scriptures?

Just as it is in any relationship, the key is communication. You
must make time to talk to God, and ask for His wisdom and understanding. Talk to Him as you would a close friend. Understanding will come in time. The more you communicate with
Him, the more understanding you will receive. In other words,
the more you draw nigh unto God, the more He will draw unto
you.

Think about it...

Choose a passage of Scripture, and ask the Lord to give you
wisdom and understanding. This can be a passage that you
have puzzled over before, or a passage that He gives you when
you begin. Take some time, and journal your revelation here.

_____

_____

_____

_____

_____

_____

_____

_____

_____

_____

_____

_____

_____

_____

Day Twenty-seven

"Likewise the Spirit helps us in our weakness. For we do not know what to pray for as we ought, but the Spirit himself intercedes for us with groanings too deep for words."
Romans 8:26 (NIV)

What do I say?

We tend to think that it's about the words that we speak— but while words are important, they are not the *most* important thing. We *must believe what we are saying*. One with faith can say very little and believe and it happens, while another without faith can say a whole lot and see nothing manifested.

Think about it...

Do you know someone who has a reputation for having their prayers answered? Have you ever listened to them as they are praying? What do you think it is about their prayers that "opens Heaven?"

_____
_____
_____
_____
_____
_____
_____
_____
_____
_____
_____
_____
_____
_____
_____
_____
_____

Day Twenty-eight

"Call to me and I will answer you, and will tell you great and hidden things that you have not known."
Jeremiah 33:3 (NIV)

Make prayer your lifeline...
When prayer becomes your lifeline, it doesn't take much to draw you in. As soon as you think of one thing you know the Lord did for you, it's enough to send you on a prayer frenzy.

What has He done for you?
Pause for a moment, and think of something that you know only the Lord could have done. Lift your hands, and tell Him "Thank you" over and over again! Sometimes, you may have to drive down memory lane. *(Do not park...you're just visiting!)*

Think about it...
Take some time now, and write a prayer of thanksgiving to the Lord for that one thing in your life that you know could not have happened without Him by your side.

_____

_____

_____

_____

_____

_____

_____

_____

_____

_____

_____

_____

_____

Day Twenty-nine

"That ye put off concerning the former conversation the old man,
which is corrupt according to the deceitful lusts; and be renewed in
the spirit of your mind; and that ye put on the new man, which after
God is created in righteousness and true holiness."
Ephesians 4:22-24 (KJV)

Replace evil with good...

There comes a time when we must make the conscious decision to get rid of our old, sinful nature and become the person that God has called us to be. While He will never force us into submission, He makes His will for our lives abundantly clear... and He's waiting for us to take action.

Think about it...

Are there parts of your life that you still need to "put off?" What are they? Are you ready to offer them to Him today and make a change? Take some time to write your thoughts here.

_____

_____

_____

_____

_____

_____

_____

_____

_____

_____

_____

_____

_____

_____

_____

_____

_____

Day Thirty

"In the same way, let your light shine before others, that they may see your good deeds and glorify your Father in heaven."
Matthew 5:16 (NIV)

Let your light shine...
You may be asking, *"How do I let my light shine?"* By setting the example! Everything must be led by prayer and love.

When you decree and declare evil, always replace it with good. For example: *"I dismantle depression, and I decree and declare that the joy of the Lord is my strength, and I have God's peace upon my life. I bind and destroy torment in my mind, and I declare and decree my mind is sound. I make sound judgments and think on things that are pure, lovely, and of good report."*

Think about it...
Write your own declaration over your life here. Then, if you are comfortable, share it with a friend.

_____

_____

_____

_____

_____

_____

_____

_____

_____

_____

_____

_____

_____

_____

_____

Space to Journal Your Thoughts

Types of Prayer

Let's begin to unlock some key principles that will help you establish a stronger, more effective prayer life.

Corporate Prayer: Joining together as the Body of Christ, whether in a church, a denomination, a country, or around the world, and praying together for the Lord to intervene.

"Lord, we come before you, asking you to heal our land. You said in your Word that if we "pray, humble ourselves, and turn from our wicked ways," then you will hear and heal our land. Lord, we need you to heal us. We humble ourselves before your mighty hand. We repent before you, Lord…forgive our sins and our sinful nature. Sweep across this land, and reveal yourself like never before. Let your light shine bright over every place of darkness. Overtake them, overwhelm them, and overcome them so that they are undone and redone. We declare and decree a reset for such a time as this. Lord, give us your plan and your purpose for our lives, and let this nation desire you. Let us put you back in your rightful place. You are the King of Kings and the Lord of Lords; the Lord strong in battle. We pull down every idol that tries to exalt itself above the Most High God. We exalt your name; may you be high and lifted up. For your Word declares if you be high and lifted, you will draw all men unto the father. In Jesus' name. Amen."

Intercessory Prayer: Praying for the Lord's favor in a certain situation, whether for yourself or for someone else.

"Lord, I come lifting up those who are lost; I ask that they experience an encounter with you. Break the bondage over their lives, in Jesus' name. Shine your light upon them. Bring hope and peace to every area of their life. Remove everything that has blinded them from your truth. Let your grace bring them in contact with those that will expose them to the love of Christ in such a manner that they accept you as their Lord and Savior. Lord, it's your will that none shall perish so we pray in accordance of your will that they come to the knowledge and understanding of who you are without shame or regret. Let your will and your will alone be done in their life. Break every stronghold over their life. Keep them safe from all manner of evil, and turn their heart of stone to a heart of flesh, making it pliable to receive you. Cause them to repent and surrender under your mighty hand. In Jesus' name. Amen."

Prayer of Supplication: Asking the Lord to give you what you need in this life: spiritually, physically, and emotionally.

"Lord, give me eyes to see beyond the natural. I need you to show me and guide me every day of my life. I need your wisdom in everything I do. Let everything that has died prematurely become alive and quickened. Incline my ears to hear and discern on another level. Keep me from all temptation. Keep my feet from stumbling, and do not allow me to slip nor slumber on this journey. Lord, I need your strength to carry on. Help me to remain focused, and bind all distractions that come to pull me off course. Forgive me if I have done anything in word or deed that was not pleasing in your sight…I repent before you now. Cause me to be sensitive to your voice in this season of my life, and push out every other voice. Help me to remain focused on you, and let me not veer to the left or right, but to keep my eyes to the hills from which comes my help. Let me remain humble in everything I do. Keep me from becoming prideful and boastful. Help me to love those who do not know what love is. Help me to show compassion to those who are lost and not judge their process. Help me to walk in my purpose and destiny. In Jesus' name. Amen."

Spiritual Warfare: Prayer that penetrates darkness and calls out evil.

"I declare and decree every cord of wickedness is being dismantled. I take full authority over every demonic stronghold and annihilate every band of wickedness. I command every illegal spirit of darkness to be shaken and destroyed. I declare and decree that evil has no control in our lives. I dismantle evil patterns and generational curses, in Jesus' name. I command any demonic chaos and drama in my life to be destroyed NOW, in the name of Jesus. I sever every familiar spirit that tries to attach itself to me and my family. I declare and decree that the lines of wicked communication concerning me, my destiny, and purpose are being interrupted NOW, in the name of Jesus. I come against any spirit of doubt and unbelief in my life that will cause me to doubt who I am in you. I bind confusion and frustration and declare that I have a sound mind. In Jesus' name. Amen."

Dying Prayer: A prayer for when you are at the end of yourself. You have cried, yelled, and prayed…and now you are at a place of no words. This is the best place to be, honestly. In this place, you have gotten beyond yourself and your emotions, and now you are in the purest place. A place of brokenness where your heart speaks. He hears your heart.

Where Do I Begin?

There is no "right" or "wrong" way to pray. I use a little formula that helps me to stay focused during prayer:

- **Exhortation**: I tell God who He is to me.

- **Thanksgiving**: I thank Him for what He has done.

- **Confession**: I confess my transgressions.

- **Supplication**: I intercede for others.

- **Petition**: I ask Him for what I need.

There is a little saying that goes something like this: *"You're the peanut to my butter…the bun to my burger…the cream in my coffee."*

You can say things like this to God:

"You are my friend, when I feel friendless…my hope, when I have no hope…my mother, when I feel motherless…my father, when I am fatherless."

Names of God

- **Abba**: Father
- **Basileus Basileon**: King of Kings
- **Jehovah Sabaoth**: The Lord of Hosts
- **El Elyon**: The Most High God
- **El Shaddai**: Lord God Almighty
- The **Author** and **Finisher** of Our Faith
- **El Olam**: The Alpha and Omega
- **Jehovah Nissi**: Miracle Worker
- **Jehovah Jireh**: My Provider
- **Bread of Life**
- **Waymaker**
- **Jehovah Shammah**: My Comforter
- **Promise Keeper**
- **Jehovah Rapha**: My Healer
- **El Roi**: The God Who Sees Me
- **Jehovah Rohi**: The Lord My Shepherd
- **Ancient of Days**
- **Chief Cornerstone**
- **Ruler**
- **Emmanuel**: God With Us
- **High Priest**
- **I Am**
- **Restorer**
- **Healer**

Power in Words

"The tongue can bring death or life, those who love to talk will reap the consequences."
Proverbs 18:21 (NIV)

Words that Dismantle Strongholds

I believe that there are certain words and phrases that dismantle strongholds; and when we use them in our prayers, heaven is called down, and angels are commanded to go to battle on our behalf.

- **Dismantle:** *"To disassemble, pull down, or take apart."* When we dismantle strongholds, they become unrecognizable and cease to exist.

- **Destroy:** *"To put an end to; extinguish. To render ineffective or useless, nullify; neutralize; invalidate. To defeat completely."* When we destroy the sin and strongholds in our lives, they are gone completely.

- **Uproot:** *"To pull out by the roots. To remove violently or tear away. To destroy or eradicate."* When we are dealing with sin in our lives and in our world, we need to get to the root if there is to be a lasting change.

- **Cast Down:** *"To throw or hurl; fling. To throw off or away."* Casting down our strongholds should be a forceful process. We are declaring that they are no longer a part of our lives.

- **Die by Fire:** Fire is all-consuming. When we command our strongholds to die by fire, we are saying that they are to be completely destroyed, with no chance to return.

Prayer is a call to action, and the use of strong action words is necessary to defeat the darkness surrounding our strongholds.

Examples include:

- ***Shatter*** *the glass ceiling over my ministry.*
- ***Smash*** *demonic idols.*
- ***Burn*** *spiritual wickedness.*

Everyone is called to pray…but not all are called to intercede for others. Some of you may have answered the call to intercessory prayer…know this: Interceding for others is truly a calling and not to be taken lightly. Sometimes, you will be called to intercede for another in the midst of walking your own difficult path—you must be willing to lay aside your own concerns and cry out to the Lord in intercession for another.

A Prayer for the Body of Christ

"Lord God, we lift up the Body of Christ to you today, and bind any attack on the church, in Jesus' name. We declare and decree we will not fear but will stand firm. Father, we know that all things work together for your good according to your purpose, so we believe that it is working even if we cannot see it. May we, your Church, trust your provision. Let your people not only be hearers in this season, but also doers that will do the work of the Lord. We declare and decree an increase in our faith, in our word, and in our relationship with you Father. Help us to walk beside one another in love. Let us have a servant's heart toward one another, and give us patience, unity, and humility. Help us to walk in peace with our fellow man. Let the Church be built on prayer, and let us remain consistent. Let the intercessors pray on another level. Allow fresh oil to flow from them, in Jesus' name. May they pray the oracles of your heart and desire for the Body of Christ. We declare and decree that the song of the Lord be released out of praise and worship, and a sound from heaven flow from the lips of your Psalmist. Through song breakthrough and deliverance shall manifest in our midst, and the atmosphere of worship will cause signs, wonders, and miracles. We declare and decree that the Word coming forth will cause a life-changing experience and that our people will not leave the same way they came. We declare and decree that the Word will cause immediate change and that the unadulterated and unfiltered Word of God will be released from your leader. We declare and decree souls saved set free and delivered on this day. In Jesus' name. Amen."

Kingdom blessings to you! I pray that this focus on prayer has not only given you insight but has blessed you as well, and that this time of devotion has given you something to look forward to in your prayer journey. I pray that you will begin to see the answers to your prayers manifest. I decree that after reading this book, the same seed that was planted in me be released unto you. *I declare and decree that there has been a leaping in your spirit that will cause you to make prayer your lifestyle from this day forward, in Jesus' name.*

"One plants, one waters, and God gives the increase."
1 Corinthians 3:7 (paraphrased)

Be blessed.

About the Author

Minister Laticia Washington Simpson is a dynamic keynote speaker, prophetic minister in the gospel, empowerment facilitator, end-time prophet, and prayer warrior, who equips and educates on the importance of prayer.

Minister Simpson is called by her own testimony to build and empower women who have been abused in any way; those who have been molested and those who have no self-worth, encouraging them to know who they are and helping them to understand that they are important, as well as letting them know that they no longer have to be a victim of their past.

For eight years, she has served with Pray Woman Pray, Inc., helping to equip women in the development of a stronger prayer life. She currently serves as a Lead Intercessor with the group.

Minister Simpson was ordained for her restoration and deliverance ministry in 2005 by Apostle Dr. Michelle Gordon of Hinesville, GA. She has a teaching certification from the Kingdom Christian Academy, a ministry of Faith Christian Center International in Leavenworth, Kansas, has led women's ministry and prayer teams, and has also taught in children's church.

She embraced the apostolic anointing five-fold ministry gifts in her life in 2012 and has been blessed to minister on numerous platforms throughout her journey. While stationed in South

Korea, she implemented a women's ministry group in March of 2015.

Minister Simpson retired in 2018 after serving in the United States Army for twenty-two years. She has been married to her husband, Delfawn, for ten years and is the mother of two beautiful children, Alearah and Jaylan, whom she loves dearly. She emphatically states that, *"My family is my first ministry."*

Contact the Author

If you would like to contact Minister Simpson, you may do so at:

Email:
Laticialsimpson@gmail.com

Facebook:
https://www.facebook.com/laticia.washington.1
(Laticia Washington Simpson)

Instagram: https://www.instagram.com/prophettothenation/
(Prophettothenation)

CPSIA information can be obtained
at www.ICGtesting.com
Printed in the USA
JSHW021318040421
13206JS00006B/155